NINE SERIES
Invisible Continents
Lesley Curwen
Tahmina Maula
Jane R. Rogers

Published by Nine Pens
2023
www.ninepens.co.uk

All rights reserved: no part of this book may be reproduced without the publisher's permission.

The rights of the authors Lesley Curwen, Tahmina Maula and Jane R. Rogers to be identified as the authors of this work has been asserted by them in accordance with the Copyright, Designs and Patents act 1988

ISBN: 978-1-7391517-3-7

NS 006

Contents

  5 Invisible Cities
  6 In which I become Plymouth Sound
  8 Missing Stitches
  9 Indian Summer (in England)
10 An Ability to Fly
12 Views of Greenland from Seat 39a
13 Holding Your Shadow
14 An Italic Tree
16 Final Arrangement
17 The Geography of Loss
18 Shotgun
19 Dolphins Sense Grief on the Water
20 When the Time Comes
21 Insomniac
22 Interpreter of Sound
23 Burnt Birdsong
24 Seaglass and Us
25 Foraminifera, Plymouth Sound
26 The Longings of the Kuiper Belt
27 Leaving
28 The Difference
29 Swimming with Octogenarians, Batten Beach
30 Migraine
31 *Mishti Brishti*
32 Take Me
33 Running Free
34 Moon, I Love You FULLY

Invisible Cities

Mother love was the country we gazed on first -
a *saree* spooling a path to the sea, an *achol*
trailing with carefree abandon - the gifts of life
flowed endlessly. Now time-zones and hemispheres
disappear at the Bay of Bengal – ancestral
homes lost on ocean breeze. In unseen gestures
something of this land of poets and dreamers endures
in me – the longing for homeland will never cease.

The heart is an arc of invisible cities that all seasons
of sea sustain. As fragments stretched
over borderlands, we inhabit the space between waking
and sleep. Memories burn bittersweet
with reminders of that place of myth – the first country –
where a fine line was drawn between our feet.

In which I become Plymouth Sound

I am we are bowl-filled-with-brine.
Together hold a kind of vastness
rimmed by breakwater, red soil.

At lowest astronomical tide
cracked teeth rise but no trace
of past journey is perceptible

except for tributes at Mayflower
steps to speculators who staged
raids across the compassed globe.

I am we are diesel-rainbow-veined
for this is true Sound, no re-touched
pic seen from a Hoe perspective.

My hair grows bladderwrack, eyes
shine nacreous, heart slides west like
the steep chevron folds in Jennycliff.

Men's effluent from frigates, trawlers
floats stinking in our face and shawls
of orange net bedeck Batten beach.

I am we are ablaze with warning signs.
At dusk channel-marks flash red/green
a toppled Xmas tree with lights still on.

Morning appears benign. We embrace
sandy kids, neoprene swimmers playing
in our high and ever higher tides.

I am we are electrolyte-sump-live
batteries built by precise accretion,
evolution mapped in every drop and cell.

We are Sound lapped in a mineral frame.
Listen to our roll, we unfold what is real.

Missing Stitches

after Alighiero Boetti's Maps

Anonymous, we worked hard,
filled the waiting material,
coaxed taut threads to the edges
of countries, indenting islands,
stabbing fabric and skin, until we made
that final stitch – cast-off at the jagged
black border of your nation's flag.

Later, I feel something is missing.
I select a sumptuous white silk –
not ordinary white, but a ghostly
no-colour for an invisible continent.
I resume work. Push needle against
these new stitches' reluctance
to join your world design. I listen
for the songs of ownership, hear
polar winds drown out all claims.

I persist in stitching the vastness
of Antarctica. Even though the violent
whites are painful to my eyes,
I am patient, skating the embroidery
through my needle's eye:
the strange journey of ice-silk
through fingers, pristine as it glistens --
weaves its own map.

Indian Summer (in England)

September swoons,
        sensuous in flames of Indian summer.
Ochre carpets roll out harvest on days that glimmer

and the nights smoulder
        beneath timeless constellations as Jaipur
shimmers upon pink sands, or in such locations

of peeling beauty
        and blustering rust, with orange burning
where leaves pirouette as the dervish whirls – each one

turning to crouch or flare.
        See October sweeping through the hedge crisp
confetti streams, 'til numb November feels for autumn's edge.

Then birds like clouds will swell,
        from nothing, to everything, in this grand farewell.

An Ability to Fly

Feet on the carpeted floor hands on the chair –

heartbeats smoulder sunrays stream through
body's hourglass energise the visible spectrum
surf waves of warmth and motion.

Speed increases with cheetah velocity –

a fast-forward hypersonic Mach warp propulsion
of the human body mind wilfully bounding onward.

In flight with an instrumental soundtrack –

reptilian thoughts jettisoned into the broody sky
to disappear beyond the Kármán line
emotions recalibrated as bright and expectant.

It takes little effort to zoom through zero gravity –

without oxygen: aerodynamic arm-wings
flap in deft acceleration defying physics
executing a front crawl through space clouds.

With laps of colour-popping earth

a meditation of colour surprises flying above yellow cities
blue oceans psychedelic reefs snow-capped mountains
volcanic eruptions green forests

an expanse of thoughts moves into a vacuum -

The residue of memory   each impossible visual
becomes a history of photons   settled back into stardust
relieved of the viewer   that made those pictures exist.

The sensuous soundtrack propels -

one instant on   into   the next into   the continuous next
image after saturated image anticipated   willed on.

Silence in a body tuned -

to nature's sounds   learning
absence   of fear's weight   accepting
touch   is what another body feels

with hands on the chair   feet on the carpeted floor.

Views of Greenland from Seat 39a

a second bloody mary crackles
I imagine bergs sweating to bits
in carbon-knit jumpers

see the curved bay blown
by a thousand jewels
spotted by slabs
linerlike   sharp prows
decks   a   mile   long
a sight to dismay lookouts
fleet with no crew   no compass
no heading   no sails

how long does it takes to melt
diamond-hard bodies   to flush them
down the bowl of Labrador Sea

who knew that dilution of water
by water would choke plankton
for want of plankton   whales expire

I am looking out for whales
they are invisible from this height
too far away to be real

Holding Your Shadow

For Abul Maula

It's the light we carry that makes us
while shadows take shape around.
But a shadow is a wing of a passing cloud.

My pockets lined with feathers fallen
from the backs of others, I follow
the scents and sounds of remembering.

The fall from grace begins the moment
you push against doors once closed, so
I no longer dream big because the fall

is too great to hold onto the dream mid-
fall. But I feel you're somewhere beside me still
because the words I choose are echoes,

because these arms left holding your shadow
aren't quite as winged as they seem.

An Italic Tree

This tree stands slant.
As the memories it holds up bear leaves,
lean its trunk to one side,

its cautious browns, sharp coppers,
fabulous bronzes,
whisper. And so, I heard it,

explored its past lives,
one life gnarled, another pruned.
Sustained with air, rain, soil, mother sun,

fragile are the hurts it wraps
in each year's ring growth,
sucking experience in, pushing age outward.

There is the break-up, there the abuses
that have left it crooked all these years.
Branched, climbed, animal-bearing,

this tree is strong. One part blooms
with green shoots,
a persistence of thoughts

in light and shade
that grow next to each other and
creak, alive in a display

of low-slung successes, easy to reach,
or higher up in the crown,
admired from a distance.

Another part is sky soaking,
with the leaves bagged and
next season already on its shoulders,

while its roots, ever growing,
are wrapping in close,
those dragged memories.

Final Arrangement

Blowsy scarlet hibiscus echoes
the satin of your cruise dress.

Freesia, a shade of mauve you chose
for my baby frock sewn

with finest needle. Most wonderful
of all, your bells of tuberose

each wax heart a scrap of bridal white
destined to turn brown and deliquesce.

These I have cut from untended beds,
blossoms dressed in a crystal vase

to be revered and tenderly
consigned to compost at the last.

The Geography of Loss

The geography of loss was the first lesson –
leave-takings on absent shores.
What-might-have-beens now lost in time
caught on the weft and warp.

Distance spins with new measures:
hour-on-hour time-travelled
saree silks by length unravelled
baganbilas, stem-by-stem,
blossoming through far-off soils.

Somewhere there's a place we count on
where the heart still feels what the eyes can't see.

Shotgun

after Yinka Shonibare sculpture,
Woman Shooting Cherry Blossoms

Markswoman, she stands in front of the target.
Feet planted, eyes focussed, shotgun raised.
And in the pause – when her head spins
with the pull of a colonial past – tension
rises inside her breasts: her feelings are ships sails
trapped in a bottle. Her skirts rustle with the weight
of stories and stones, her breaths draw in the batik that clings
to the stance of her hips. And her emotions grow
into her hands. She holds the shotgun steady.
In that moment she squeezes the trigger.
And in the ricochet of her shot,
as smoke clears – from the gun's barrels
spring cherry blossoms – explosions
of blush, coral, ballet-slipper pink.

Dolphins Sense Grief on the Water

glittersplash   here they fly
  drawn to   grave distress
   glossy backs   spinning light

four bow   in honour of my loss
 spear upward   clear of green seas
  weave alongside   hold my gaze

       unbearably alive

 on ocean's face   they write strange equations
in sun and breath   teach me the finite value
 of moments   pinsharp sting of happiness

When the Time Comes

                let me be rocked on deck
           weightless on sea-breast
       imperceptible roll and sway
             gift of yesterday's storm-wave

remember how you and I
    plaited arms half-asleep
        drifting on the boat's heft
minds doused in wordlessness

                let me be rapt on deck
          folded in slow build
       and hold   inevitable
        fall
              fearless calm
     in muscle, ear and
 eye

  no arms around me now
but faithful sea   a boat-skin
     close to mine   infinite
         quiet of being held

  bodyless
      in oceanic night

Insomniac

At midnight the mind expands, becomes a wakeful mosaic;
the bedroom a war zone: hybrid of project sleep and mania.
At 1.am, a hot drink, the cereal packet; riboflavin and niacin,
magic ingredients for sleep. At 2.am, a solitary moan;
police siren at a distance. At 3.am, the city faints, its main
distractions asleep. The bed shrinks. Hard stone, its mason
has carved a ridged walnut shell to lie in. Anon,
the flawed artistry of rest, a scrutiny of listening; coin
of many, many more minutes worshipping the icon
Sleep. At 5.am, the welcome glimpse of sunrise; a scion
of daylight in which to plan the next moments of insomnia.

Interpreter of Sound

Interpreter of sound I am pure bone and gesture
learning to dream in my mother-tongue.
Language of place laps fresh and gentle
as lake sounds and the springtime call
of the *kukil*. Rickshaws trundle city streets
and laneways, vie with the *phut-phut* of *CNGs*.
A street hawker, amidst the bustle,
is caught in the spell of the *muezzin*.

Through *Grishma's* heat the rice-paper beat
of a *projapothi* – bearing souls
to other worlds. It swoops then sweeps
ineffably through the veined city.
Warm memories stir on the rub of a breeze –
a distant land still communes with me.

Burnt Birdsong

A cold afternoon, an old room, *her*,
kneeling at the fireplace, burnt letters
leftover in the grate, now in her hands.
Between scorch marks, some stirring words
are easy to make out. She reads aloud
letters between lovers, about their affair.
They'd tried to destroy evidence, *yet,*

their written breath is birdsong:
staves of melody flying over pylon lines,
calling for food, for sex. Wings ripple
out on a thermal of air, an undulation,
from texture of paper to tenure of prayer.
She closes her eyes, knees pressed to the grate,
her shaky fingers hold on to a human story.

Seaglass and Us

  edges mashed   borders milled to dust
  spun like atoms   crushed to
  something
    else

  clear turns opaque   sharp turns blunt
  shrinkage time-lapse-fast   erosion
  never
   stops

  damaged goods   sanded to cabochon
  debris reborn   morphs to
  stranded
   gem

Foraminifera, Plymouth Sound

Curled shell whisker-wide discloses filaments seeking
to engulf algae, bacteria.   Ameboid, single-celled
all but
                          invisible.

Your ancestors form galaxies in Giza's stone.
Sand/calcite secreted in snailish whorls
coiled rigid as a nut
                          or human skull.

Stranded at bitter-end of food chains, prey
to tiny mouths.   Worms, bivalves, crustaceans
suck your
                          plasmic juice.

Short-lived, loved only by geologists as microscopic
clocks, your loss is measured in pollution graphs.
Millions pulped
                          in floor-mush.

All but invisible, these ciliate arms may touch
me as I swim, you who are nothing to us
and also
                          every thing.

The Longings of the Kuiper Belt

On the cold fringes, slung
from the violent mash-up
of creation, orbiting
as foreign correspondents of Neptune –
with a certain *sang-froid* –
we were the excluded.

With discretion – in our exiled years –
we shivered in the dark maw
of the outer Solar System,
working our icy rubble, waiting
till your fire-faiths
cooled to logic.

Curious then,
you appreciated (not feared),
the dirty snowballs we nudged
in your direction. And at last, looking
through the snowy bedcovers
of distance, away from your noisy Sun

your saw us: the invisible.
Finally, time melted as you
tuned to our exotic voices
named us – comets –
fulfilling our prediction, of knowing
you loved us, long before we were claimed.

Leaving

You're leaving again, slipping away to shadow.
Headlights flood the road ahead, cutting
through *koo-washa* – a winter mist – that
shrouds the city in ghostly streams. The air
stirs, perhaps on the whir of the *shalik's* wing.
Hasna hena – night-blooming jasmine – bows
to dawn, drowsy with sleep. Inside the car
your *kameez* clings, the voile gathered against

your skin. First light veils the fingernail
moon. The stars wash away. All wonder done.
I picture you still, though your image fades
into the crosshatch of empty streets.
Your voice grows smaller with every distance.
The wail of the heart like a wild cat on heat.

The Difference

after Robert Frost

don't you feel, there exists somewhere a road not taken
    one filled with the song of the *bulbuli*
where a slatted bridge leads over a pond towards
    woodlands of *shalbon* and *shegun* trees

where villagers bathe in cool waters   free from the toil
 of the paddy fields   there is the place of rain-filled air
of morning star   evening sky of rustic greys   a landscape
  born of spellbound bullocks   where *palli barsha* brings
  monsoon upland lowland   to sun-splashed hillocks

beyond the groves shutters wide   a breeze teases
    moonlight pools in meditation   deep in this land of
mist and tide framed by twists of *bokul-phul*   rivers
    curve and seasons guide   dreams ploughed deep
in field and forest   *jamuna*   *surma* stream their light

along these trails hear laughter rise   arias on summer air
        sweet wonder at the road not taken.

Swimming with Octogenarians, Batten Beach

We change at the sea wall. Shiver as we grope
and wriggle into costumes, flailing on one leg.
Comical in Mickey Mouse gloves, baggy flesh.
Some swimmers are deaf; I cup hands, yell against
the wind or lean close. Six feet apart is hard to do.

One recent widow (eighty-three) wants a solid arm
to lean on, wading over pebbles, bladderwrack.
We trudge in like ancient crabs, accept the pain
of entry calm, unstunned. Then feet kick free
we are seals soaring through our own domain.

Years fall away, death and shore recede.
Skin stretched salt-tight, hearts unsore,
nothing exists but body and freezing sea.

Migraine

It made its first appearance as a distinctive Gamine,
doe-eyed, slim-built; tapping out a routine of mini
dance steps in warning. It wore an ominous name,
soon became more savage in shape, clicked up a gear,
took on the guise of a Matador working the ring.
Dazzling in resplendent brocade, amidst the bloody game
it partnered a stamping bull, fuelling its rage.
Shapeshifting after the kill, it fixed form as a Miner
pounding out strong laboured blows; a pulsing image
reverberating with thud, hack, thud. I endure its reign
in a concentration of tender hurt, as its pick's range
hews at my head. If I become Sleep, I'll escape its anger.

Mishti Brishti

Between homeland and sky there is a place that
comes and goes - a brigadoon of flat-earth textures
green and gold. Luscious, nebulous, at times
exalting! The days we watched, we breathed, we sighed
how good it felt to be alive in the *borsha-kal*
with the sweet, wild tang of *rajoni gandha*,
kamranga and the pungent peel of *lebu rosha*.
Here, the queen of fruit, like nectar blooms
with honey-soft, apricot ooze. *Rhimi-*

jhimi, mishti brishti, a forgotten yearning
for sweet monsoon. *Brishti pore tappur-*
tuppur; splish-splash against the awnings
of painted rickshaws, spilling gladly over
the pavements of Elephant Road. Everywhere
the tiny beads fall *tip-tip*, spitting
up as hot oil from a pan. Deep in the ears
a rhythm drums *dhol-dhol* pounding
over lily-pads, bouncing and skimming

village ponds. Rain rain gathering
pace; tapping its feet in impatient flurries;
glass-heeled rain-drops strike *thung-thung* over
tin-rooves from Sylhet's tea gardens to boundless
shores of Cox's Bazaar. *Brishti pore*
thale-thale; revellers dance with carefree
rhythm beneath warm showers. Rain to wash sins,
all fears, all cares. This life-giving pulse.
These glorious days!

Take Me

shall we
(not) return one day
for the love of homeland
is on the air of each breath
we take

                        take me
              back to the places
          of our formative years
            to reclaim the light
                 of lost days

Running Free

rippled mane spits white beads
sun gifts endless diamond
        flash on stippled flow

sheets pulled iron taut
a cloud-quilt shadows Plymouth
        slides south to Spain

my boat tips and yaws
I ride her like a gaucho
        rockinghorsebronco

through seas finite but giant
a cornflowerblue royal robe
        to cool a planet

my love and I plough through
plastic, oil-slicks, submarines
        shit, bodies, melted ice

fleets of sardine, shark
whale and cell-wide life in
        celebration, grief, what you will

Moon, I Love You FULLY

Wolf (old/ice) –
in the changing room I unpack myself

Snow (storm/hunger) –
on a whim I experiment with a willingness to cry

Worm (chaste/death/crust/sap) –
I check the flow of blood to my limbs

Pink (sprouting grass/egg/fish) –
only I, try to glide on crows' breath

Flower (hare/corn planting/milk) –
only I, dance like a butterfly shaking off rust

Strawberry (rose/hot) –
before long it's time to check if my soul is waterproof

Buck (hay) –
in the park I regret those blades of grass stomped on

Sturgeon (green corn/grain/red) –
carried away I throw my last bathing suit into the trees

Full Corn (barley/harvest) –
in the cafe I smoke a pipe which raises eyebrows

Hunter's (travel/dying grass) –
in the moment I cut back dead roses I am called insightful

Beaver (frost) –
when the water is deep enough, I bury my treasure

Cold (long night/oak) –
the kissing gate is a border and I forget to kiss you

The Poets

Lesley Curwen is a broadcaster, poet and sailor living within sight of Plymouth Sound. She often writes about sailing, loss, and the environmental damage done to the oceans and their wildlife. Her poems have been published (or soon will be) by Broken Sleep, The Storms, Arachne Press, Black Bough, Ice Floe Press, Iamb Poetry and After Poetry.

Poems:

6   In which I become Plymouth Sound
12 Views of Greenland from Seat 39a
16 Final Arrangement
19 Dolphins Sense Grief on the Water
20 When the Time Comes
24 Seaglass and Us
25 Foraminifera, Plymouth Sound
29 Swimming with Octogenarians, Batten Beach
33 Running Free

Acknowledgements:

'Views of Greenland from Seat 39a' published in 'Words from the Brink' by Arachne Press 2021

'In which I become Plymouth Sound' published in 'Footprints – an anthology of New Ecopoetry' by Broken Sleep 2022

'Swimming with Octogenarians' published in 'Quay Voices #1' by Impress Books 2021

Tahmina Maula is a British-Bengali poetry and prose writer. She is an EAP Lecturer and has done freelance work for The Poetry Society. Her current writing interests include language, memory and loss. She lives in Greenwich, London.

Poems:

- 5 Invisible Cities
- 9 Indian Summer (in England)
- 13 Holding your Shadow
- 17 The Geography of Loss
- 22 Interpreter of Sound
- 27 Leaving
- 28 The Difference
- 31 *Mishti Brishti*
- 32 Take Me

Jane R Rogers is a poet, knitter, and a book production specialist in the publishing industry. She is currently working on a sequence of poems inspired by ice cores and often writes in the 'A Gram of &'s' form. Her poems have appeared in Envoi, Prole, The Curlew, Long Exposure Magazine, Tears in the Fence, among others. She lives in Lewisham, London.

Poems:

8   Missing Stitches
10 An Ability to Fly
14 An Italic Tree
18 Shotgun
21 Insomniac
23 Burnt Birdsong
26 The Longings of the Kuiper Belt
30 Migraine
34 Moon, I Love You FULLY

Acknowledgements:

'Missing Stitches' first appeared in Poetry from Art online 2012, at Tate Modern.

Jane, Tahmina and Lesley would like to thank the members of Greenwich Poetry Workshop for their feedback and friendship.

www.ingramcontent.com/pod-product-compliance
Lightning Source LLC
Chambersburg PA
CBHW021134080526
44587CB00012B/1286